GOOD SECRETS,
BAD SECRETS

Deborah J. Monroe

LifeRich Publishing is a registered trademark of The Reader's Digest Association, Inc.

LifeRich Publishing books may be ordered through booksellers or by contacting:

LifeRich Publishing
1663 Liberty Drive
Bloomington, IN 47403
www.liferichpublishing.com
1 (888) 238-8637

Because of the dynamic nature of the Internet, any web addresses or links contained in this book may have changed since publication and may no longer be valid. The views expressed in this work are solely those of the author and do not necessarily reflect the views of the publisher, and the publisher hereby disclaims any responsibility for them.

Any people depicted in stock imagery provided by Thinkstock are models, and such images are being used for illustrative purposes only. Certain stock imagery © Thinkstock.

ISBN: 978-1-4897-0333-0 (sc)
ISBN: 978-1-4897-0332-3 (e)

Printed in the United States of America.

LifeRich Publishing rev. date: 11/06/2014

DEDICATION

This book is dedicated to my sons, Drew and DJ,
my nieces, nephews and every boy and girl in this world.

PREFACE

When I talk to parents about abuse, I often hear them say, "It's hard to talk about that with my child", or they ask, "Is it too early to have those talks?" Some do not want to ask because they are afraid of the answer. This is why I wrote GOOD SECRETS, BAD SECRETS. I wanted a book that would be a conversation starter for parents or caregivers who do not know how to address these issues.

This is Jody. He was told to keep a secret.

A secret is something that is not to be told to others.

Let's help Jody learn if a secret is good or bad.

Drew's dad bought his mom a ring for Mother's Day. This is a good secret.

Sarah's mom is getting her brother a puppy for doing well in school. This is a good secret.

Nate's family is giving his granddad a surprise birthday party. This is a good secret.

Mr. Smith touched Julie in a bad way. This is a bad secret.

The babysitter's boyfriend hits her. This is a bad secret.

Toby doesn't have food at home. This is a bad secret.

Good secrets make you happy and are okay to keep.
They do not hurt you or others.

Bad secrets hurt and they make you sad.
If you know a bad secret, you should tell an adult.

Are you keeping a bad secret?

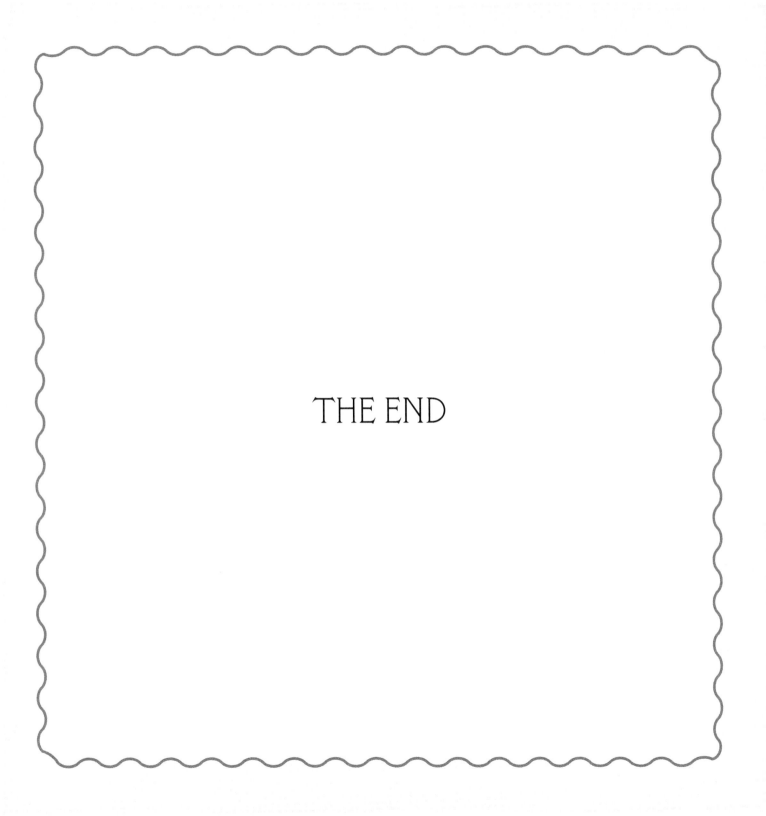

THE END

CPSIA information can be obtained
at www.ICGtesting.com
Printed in the USA
BVHW021311240720
584618BV00011B/131